KU-725-077

Make a Face

Allan Ahlberg

Colin McNaughton

Frog
Boy + Boy
Make a Face
Legs

WALKER BOOKS
LONDON

ER.
7.3.95
CITY OF COVENTRY
SCHOOLS
LIBRARY
SERVICE
LIBRARIES
JWs

First published 1985 by
Walker Books Ltd
87 Vauxhall Walk
London SE11 5HJ

This edition published 1987
Reprinted 1989, 1993

Text © 1985 Allan Ahlberg
Illustrations © 1985 Colin McNaughton

Printed in Italy by Graphicom Srl

British Library Cataloguing in Publication Data
A catalogue record for this book is
available from the British Library.
ISBN 0-7445-1014-7

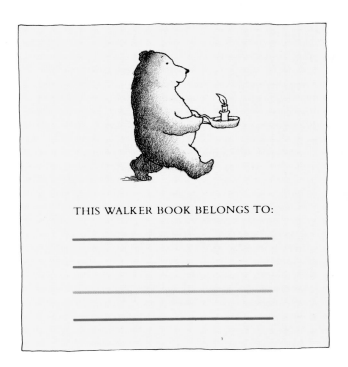

THIS WALKER BOOK BELONGS TO:

_____

_____

_____

_____

M B C

red nose readers

Frog

a frog

a big frog

a big
fat frog

a spotty big fat frog

a lumpy spotty
big fat frog...

…with a hat on

Boy + Boy

sun + sea

+ bucket + spade

+ shells + sand

+ ball + ice-cream

+ donkeys

= holidays

flower + water = big flower

pig + dinner = big pig

boy + boy + boy + boy

+ boy + boy + boy + boy

+ boy + boy + boy + boy

+ boy + boy + boy =

a pile of boys

Make a Face

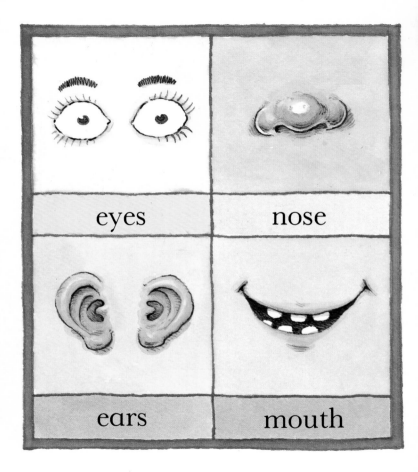

eyes	nose
ears	mouth

make a

face

chips

eggs

cake

apple

make a

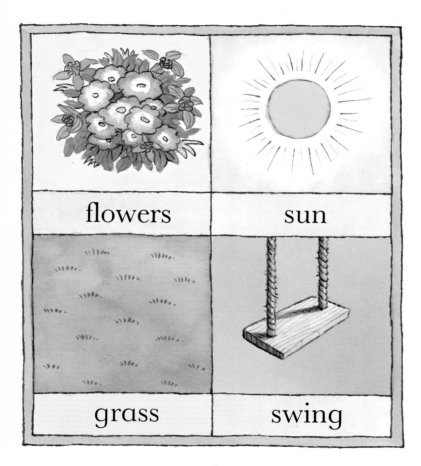

flowers

sun

grass

swing

make a

garden

| toothbrush | teddy |
| slippers | stairs |

make a

bedtime...

Legs

one leg

two legs

three legs

four legs

five legs

six legs

lift off!

the end

red nose readers

3 8002 00993 2924

Significant Author

Red Nose Readers are the easiest of easy readers – and the funniest!
Red for single words and phrases. Yellow for simple sentences.
Blue for memorable rhymes. How many have you got?

RED BOOKS

0-7445-1015-5	Bear's Birthday	£2.25
0-7445-1021-X	Big Bad Pig	£1.99
0-7445-1499-1	Fee Fi Fo Fum	£2.25
0-7445-1498-3	Happy Worm	£2.25
0-7445-1496-7	Help!	£2.25
0-7445-1497-5	Jumping	£2.25
0-7445-1014-7	Make a Face	£2.25
0-7445-1016-3	So Can I	£2.25

YELLOW BOOKS

0-7445-1700-1	Crash! Bang! Wallop!	£2.25
0-7445-1701-X	Me and My Friend	£2.25
0-7445-1020-1	Push the Dog	£1.99
0-7445-1019-8	Shirley's Shops	£1.99

BLUE BOOKS

0-7445-1703-6	Blow Me Down!	£2.25
0-7445-1702-8	Look Out for the Seals!	£2.25
0-7445-1018-X	One, Two, Flea!	£1.99
0-7445-1017-1	Tell Us A Story	£2.25

**Walker Paperbacks are available from most booksellers, or by post from
Walker Books Ltd, PO Box 11, Falmouth, Cornwall TR10 9EN.**

To order, send: title, author, ISBN number and price for each book ordered, your full name and address and
a cheque or postal order for the total amount, plus postage and packing:
UK and BFPO Customers – £1.00 for first book, plus 50p for the second book and plus 30p for each
additional book to a maximum charge of £3.00.
Overseas and Eire Customers – £2.00 for first book, plus £1.00 for the second book and plus 50p per copy for each additional l
Prices are correct at time of going to press, but are subject to change without notice.